JOSEPH MIDTHUN   SAMUEL HITI

BUILDING BLOCKS OF SCIENCE

THE CELL CYCLE

WORLD
BOOK

a Scott Fetzer company
Chicago

www.worldbook.com

World Book, Inc.
180 North LaSalle Street
Suite 900
Chicago, Illinois 60601
USA

For information about other World Book publications,
visit our website at **www.worldbook.com**
or call **1-800-WORLDBK (967-5325).**
For information about sales to schools and libraries,
call 1-800-975-3250 (United States),
or 1-800-837-5365 (Canada).

Library of Congress Cataloging-in-Publication Data
The cell cycle.
        pages cm. -- (Building blocks of science)
    Summary: "A graphic nonfiction volume that
introduces plant and animal cells and their cycles,
including cell diagrams, meiosis, mitosis, and
disease"-- Provided by publisher.
    Includes index.
    ISBN 978-0-7166-2828-6
    1. Cytology--Juvenile literature. 2. Cells--Juvenile
literature. I. World Book, Inc.
    QH582.5.C45 2014
    571.6--dc23
                                2014004710

Building Blocks of Science, Set 2
ISBN: 978-0-7166-2820-0 (set, hc.)

Also available as:
ISBN: 978-0-7166-7887-8 (pbk.)
ISBN: 978-0-7166-7879-3 (trade, hc.)
ISBN: 978-0-7166-2962-7 (e-book, EPUB3)

Printed in China by Shenzhen Donnelley
Printing Co., Ltd., Guangdong Province
2nd printing December 2016

STAFF
Executive Committee
President: Jim O'Rourke
Vice President and Editor in Chief:
    Paul A. Kobasa
Vice President, Finance: Donald D. Keller
Vice President, Marketing: Jean Lin
Vice President, International Sales:
    Maksim Rutenberg
Director, Human Resources: Bev Ecker

Editorial
Director, Digital & Print Content Development:
    Emily Kline
Editor, Digital & Print Content Development:
    Kendra Muntz
Editor, Life Sciences: Jacqueline Jasek
Manager, Indexing Services: David Pofelski
Manager, Contracts & Compliance
    (Rights & Permissions): Loranne K. Shields
Writer and Letterer: Joseph Midthun

Digital
Director, Digital Product Development:
    Erika Meller
Digital Product Manager: Lyndsie Manusos

Manufacturing/Pre-Press
Production/Technology Manager:
    Anne Fritzinger
Proofreader: Nathalie Strassheim

Graphics and Design
Senior Art Director: Tom Evans
Coordinator, Design Development and
    Production: Brenda B. Tropinski
Book Design: Samuel Hiti

Acknowledgments:
Created by Samuel Hiti and Joseph Midthun
Art by Samuel Hiti
Text by Joseph Midthun
Special thanks to Syril McNally

TABLE OF CONTENTS

There is a glossary on page 30. Terms defined in the glossary are in type **that looks like this** on their first appearance.

Most white blood cells live about 13 days, while red blood cells live about 120 days.

Nerve cells might live up to 100 years.

In the plant kingdom, death is somewhat different.

Sometimes, plant cells seem to live until they are no longer needed by the plant.

However, if this flower doesn't get enough water...

...entire **structures**, like leaves, or even the stem, can wither and die.

Flop

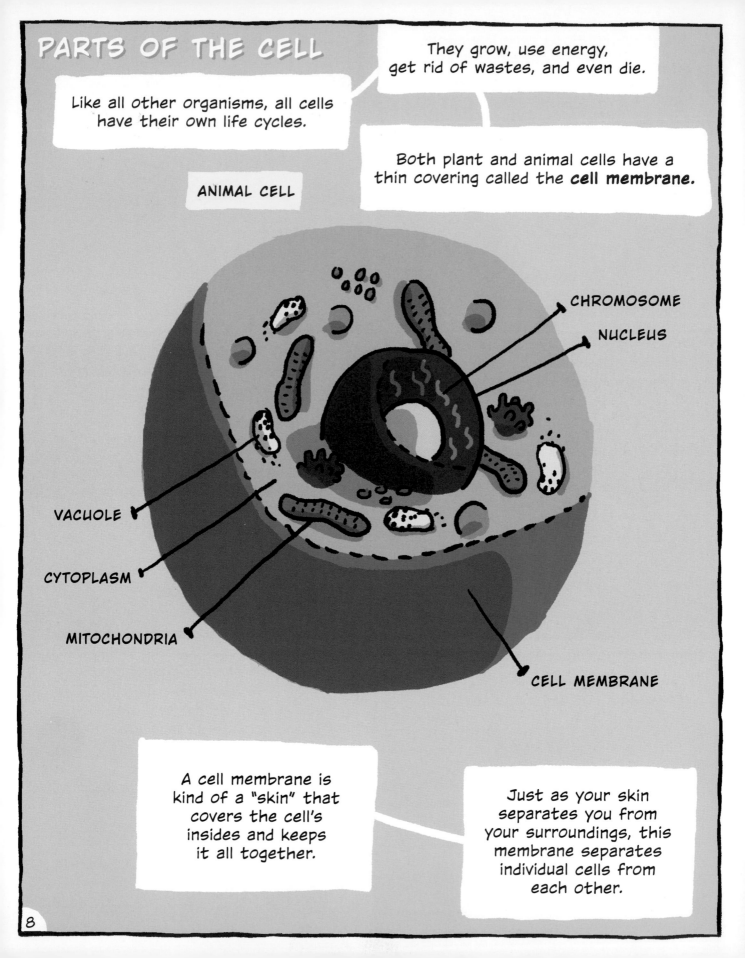

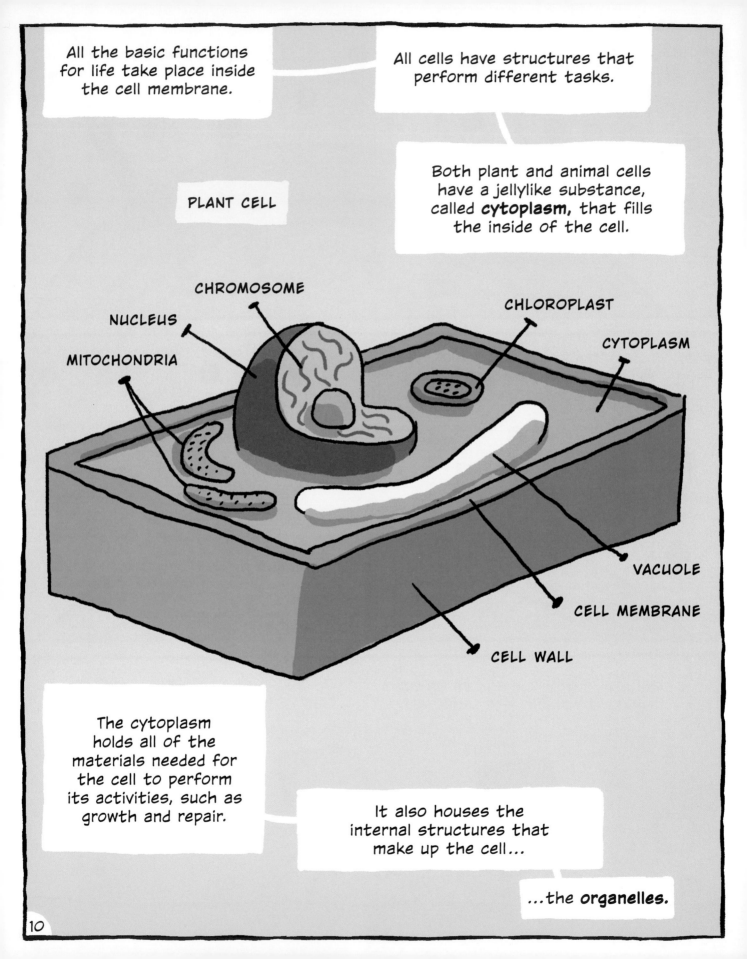

Plant and animal cells both use energy from food to live.

Inside a cell, food is turned into energy by organelles called **mitochondria.**

The mitochondria are the power plants of the cell.

Chemical reactions inside these organelles transform food into energy.

The cell can then use the energy to perform different life functions, such as getting rid of wastes.

Cells use energy to work together to perform important functions—

pant pant

—like breathing!

IMPORTANT DIFFERENCES

But, remember, for all the similarities between their cells, you can usually tell by looking at them that...

First, plant cells have some structures that animal cells do not.

...animal cells and plant cells are not exactly the same.

These structures can help us tell the difference between plant and animal cells.

Plant cells have important differences from animal cells.

Parts of the Cell	Animal Cells	Plant Cells
Cell membrane	✓	✓
Cell wall		✓
Chloroplasts		✓
Chromosomes	✓	✓
Cytoplasm	✓	✓
Mitochondria	✓	✓
Nucleus	✓	✓
Vacuole	many small	few large

While most animal cells usually have a round shape, all plant cells have an additional stiff covering outside the cell membrane called—

—the cell wall!

WHOA!

GLOSSARY

atom the basic unit of matter.

cancer a disease marked by an out-of-control growth of body cells.

cell the basic unit of all living things.

cell division the process by which cells split and make new cells.

cell membrane a covering that separates the inside of a cell from the outside environment.

cell wall the stiff covering outside of the cell membrane in a plant cell.

chlorophyll the green pigment in plant cells that helps with photosynthesis.

chloroplast the "food factory" in a plant cell.

chromosomes tiny threadlike strands that carry genes.

cytokinesis a process of cell division in which the cytoplasm divides to make two new cells.

cytoplasm the material that fills a cell.

daughter cells the new cells formed as a result of cell division.

DNA the chainlike structures found in cells that direct cell formation and growth.

egg the female reproductive cell.

fertilization the process by which a male sperm cell and a female egg cell join together.

gametes an organism's sex cells.

life cycle the stages that a living thing goes through as it develops.

meiosis a special type of cell division in sex cells.

mitochondria the "power plants" of a cell.

mitosis the process by which the nucleus divides and forms two identical nuclei in two new cells.

nuclear division a process of cell division in which the nucleus divides.

nucleus; nuclei the "control center" of a cell; more than one nucleus.

organ a special group of cells that work together to help the body function.

organelle a structure within the cell that has a specific job.

organism any living thing.

photosynthesis the process by which plants make their own food.

reproduce the way living things make more of their own kind.

sexual reproduction the process by which organisms produce offspring with sperm cells and egg cells.

sperm the male reproductive cell.

structure a body part of a living thing.

tumor an abnormal buildup and growth of cells on a body part.

vacuole a storage space in a cell.

virus a tiny substance that causes certain illnesses.

FIND OUT MORE

Books

All About Mitosis and Meiosis
by Elizabeth R. Mankato Cregan
(Compass Point, 2010)

Cell
by Richard Spilsbury and
Louise Spilsbury
(Heinemann Library, 2014)

Cell Biology
by Aubrey Stimola
(Rosen Central, 2011)

Cells
by Susan Meredith
(Rourke, 2010)

Cells Up Close
by Maria Nelson
(Gareth Stevens, 2014)

Inheritance and Reproduction
by Jen Green
(Capstone Heinemann Library, 2014)

The Manga Guide to Biochemistry
by Takemura, Masaharu, and Kikuyar
(No Starch Press, 2011)

Websites

BBC Bitesize Science: What's in a Cell?
http://www.bbc.co.uk/schools
/gcsebitesize/science/add_edexcel
/cells/cells1.shtml
The structures, features, and
functions of cells are examined in a
short unit, complete with diagrams
and boldface key terms.

BBC Bitesize Science: Mitosis and Meiosis
http://www.bbc.co.uk/schools
/gcsebitesize/science/add_edexcel/cells
/mitosisact.shtml
Find out why cell division is so important
during reproduction in this narrated
activity.

BBC Bitesize Science: Cells to Systems
http://www.bbc.co.uk/bitesize/ks3
/science/organisms_behaviour_health
/cells_systems/revision/1/
Read about plant and animal cell functions
and then complete an animated instruc-
tional video and a multiple-choice test.

Centre of the Cell: All About Cells
http://www.centreofthecell.org
/centre/?page_id=1&ks=2
Take an in-depth look at animal cells and
examine the life inside your cells.

Centre of the Cell: Games and Interactives
http://www.centreofthecell.org/games/
Select a topic to play a clickable game,
or explore a 3D cell model to learn more
about their function in your body.

Nobelprize.org: Control of the Cell Cycle
http://www.nobelprize.org/educational
/medicine/2001/cellcycle.html
Become a Cell Division Supervisor as you
enter the nucleus and guide the cell
through the phases of cell division.

Nova Online: How Cells Divide
http://www.pbs.org/wgbh/nova/body
/how-cells-divide.html
Travel into the tiny world of cells and
explore cell division with interactive,
animated diagrams.

PBS LearningMedia: Cell Division
http://www.pbslearningmedia.org
/resource/lsps07.sci.life.stru.celldivision
/cell-division/
Learn why cells are critical to life on
Earth in this step-by-step examination
of cell division, with bonus discussion
questions.

INDEX